ONE HUNDRED WAYS TO

Live with a
Cat Addict

ONE HUNDRED WAYS TO

Live with a Cat Addict

BY

Ronald Payne

ILLUSTRATIONS BY

Jilly Wilkinson

Hodder & Stoughton
LONDON SYDNEY AUCKLAND

Text copyright © 2004 by Ronald Payne
Illustrations copyright © 2004 by Jilly Wilkinson

First published in Great Britain in 2004

The right of Ronald Payne to be identified as the Author of
the Work has been asserted by him in accordance with the
Copyright, Designs and Patents Act 1988.

10 9 8 7 6 5 4 3 2 1

British Library Cataloguing in Publication Data
A record for this book is available from
the British Library

ISBN 0 340 86343 9

Typeset in Baskerville by Avon DataSet Ltd,
Bidford-on-Avon, Warwickshire

Printed and bound in Great Britain by
Bookmarque Ltd, Croydon, Surrey

The paper and board used in this paperback are natural
recyclable products made from wood grown in sustainable
forests. The manufacturing processes conform to the
environmental regulations of the country of origin.

Hodder & Stoughton
A Division of Hodder Headline Ltd
338 Euston Road
London NW1 3BH
www.madaboutbooks.com

To my wife, Celia Haddon, with love.

It is the task of those who live with cat addicts
to protect the protectors – sometimes even
from themselves.

Contents

For Starters (or the Age of Innocence)

The origin of *One Hundred Ways to Live with a Cat Addict* lies in a matrimonial crisis provoked by feline perversity, during which an ultimatum was issued:

'Either that cat goes, or I do!'

'Right!' said Celia, lips pursed.

Nothing much happened.

Nearly a couple of decades later the pet peril, Fat Ada, a Victorian parlour maid among cats, passed away peacefully, still a respected member of the family.

My wife is comparable to the sort of woman who becomes pregnant at the first kiss. Figuratively, she has kittens. I once joked that she is so addicted to them that if she so much as approached a hedge or bush in the country, some eager four-legged orphan would leap into her arms.

Within days, on Christmas Eve for good measure, such a scene was actually played out in a Somerset lane. That called for quick thinking. Stroking the small head, I suggested that it probably belonged to the nearby farm I had spotted. In no time it was restored to a joyful child owner. In a fit of relief and gratitude, I dashed the kid a fiver.

Brought up in innocence in a totally pet-free environment, the only fact I learned about the creatures came from my first reading lesson. 'The cat sat on the mat,' it announced. But so for that matter did the dog.

All that changed when I married into the petocracy. For self-protection a feline crash course became essential – quickly followed by how to manage the surprises, perils and delights of living with a woman devoted to cats.

Addicts and How to Cope with Them

Fifteen thousand years of history are looking down on the cato-human relationship. Don't mess with it!

Truly it has been said that any-
one who wishes to live happily
with a devoted cat-lover must first
learn the black art of wrangling cats.
Real delight may only be achieved
by the simultaneous manipulation
of humans and cats. This is known
as the Trojan Cat Syndrome.

Ask whether any cat-sitter, pro-
fessional, relative or amateur,
is worthy of total trust to perform
all the tasks of care and maintenance demanded by the companion pet. If the answer is not one,
then your partner is an addict and
might just as well call out, 'My
name is X and I'm a cat addict.'

We must face the tragic fact that many people fail to understand that they have become addicts. Just as hardened alcoholics say they are 'social drinkers' or 'enjoy a glass of two', so your cat-crazed companion may admit only to being fond of the animals: 'We only have a few cats at home.'

I t is important to remember that cat addiction is a disease, though not one that can be cured by taking pills or consulting the local doctor. In fact, conventional medicine is powerless in face of the troublesome, though mercifully not immediately life-threatening, affliction.

T rying to control the loved one's addiction oneself does not work; even worse, it exhausts you. Recognition of the problem and self-help provide the only hope. Be kind and tolerant, and remember: when they lie to you, they are lying to themselves.

Addiction is a mental obsession allied to a behavioural dysfunction. Coming off it is as painful as coming off drugs. 'Cold kitten', it has been called – the equivalent of 'cold turkey'.

The more time you live in a cat-infested area, the greater the conviction takes hold that cats are addicts too. They are addicted to people.

So stand by for the big clash of addict v. addict.

Know Your Enemy

Rule one: pretend you agree.

When in doubt, suppress or at least postpone any unkind reaction that would offer even the slightest hint of any anti-feline attitude in thought, word or deed. Then surrender.

Remember: the presumption in cat-prompted conflict is that you are judged guilty of catist behaviour if any other person, or any member of the feline community, deems what you have said or done to have caused offence. In that case you have committed an offence.

The fundamental principle of rubbing along with cat or cats and devoted proprietor is to acknowledge that they are right in all circumstances. The good news is that through diplomatic negotiation a peace process may allow you to give in graciously while enjoying the honours of war.

Ignore the temptations of a third way. Emulate the crafty lawyer: accept the law, then finesse it to your own advantage.

Here is an example. Devotee: 'I'm worried about Tibbles; she seems very unhappy and listless.

The vet says she's not ill, though she left food in her bowl. Do you think she may be lonely? Wouldn't it be nice for her if we got another kitten?' This ends in a trailing question mark, as though expecting a harsh negative, or at best a vague positive.

Do not be fooled into believing

that a real consultation is taking place. Any opposition to the plan will only hasten its execution. The correct response is shared anxiety. You too should endorse worries about Tibbles' state of mind, then try to sow seeds of doubt:

'It would be lovely to have another cat, maybe a nice kitten. [Learn to lie with a smile.] The only thing is [hesitate], I just wonder if the introduction of another cat might make her feel she was being replaced. That could be deeply upsetting for such a sensitive creature.'

U nderstand that whenever your partner says in a special soft voice, 'Darling, come here. I really love you!', she or he is almost certainly addressing the cat. Learn to live with this.

B e grateful that when the fanatic in momentary anger addresses the cat: 'You really are a tiresome little person,' it is not aimed at you.

L earn the valuable skill of diverting attention from what might otherwise turn into a rela-tionship destroyer. If calamity threatens, try the tension breaker sometimes called the Mogg Move, in honour of an actual cat. She specialised in early reveille calls done by loudly scratching the bed head. One such pre-dawn foray was wrecked by the addict's partner shouting, 'At the third scratch it will be 5.43 precisely.'

Naming and Homing

Take part with enthusiasm yet caution in choosing the name of a new cat. The main aim must be to prevent it being called something embarrassing or too fanciful, like Cleopatra or Marmaduke. Never forget that the time will surely come when you will be discovered in the street by night shouting out for an errant cat with 'Come here, Marmaduke.' If possible stick to something simple like Sam or Mary.

Literary men do not set a good example. Here is Robert Southey awarding his cat a whole Almanac de Gotha of titles: 'The Most Noble the Archduke Rumpelstilzchen, Marquis Macbum, Earl Tomelmange, Baron, Raticide, Waowhler, and Skaratch.' This joke aristo-cat was buried in an orchard with catnip planted on his grave in 1833 – and not before time. T.S. Eliot, 'Tom' as we know him in feral circles, wrote of a mystery cat called Macavity, and the American poet Don Marquis recorded the sordid tale of Mehitabel: 'It's a hell of a life, Archie, but always the lady.' If your fanatic partner has literary tastes, point him/her away from any high-flown ideas when it comes to the naming of cats.

Just supposing that your addict is thoughtful enough to consult you, the non-believer, on the thorny question of what kind of cat to choose, watch out. Here be dangers!

Score useful save-the-under-privileged points by suggesting it should be acquired from Cats Protection rather than bought through vulgar commerce. Then argue for a mixed-parentage number of low birth, rather than a delicate Persian of higher lineage than the late Shah. The advantage is twofold: the statement 'I am egalitarian', and the fact that a street cat will be free and cheaper to maintain.

Display your expertise by reminding the enthusiast that long-haired cats need much more human grooming to keep them hairball free, otherwise they are often sick over the best chair. Also, these cats distribute enough surplus hair to knit a pullover a month.

Take note: I myself blundered when led to a Cats Protection joint and given as a treat the opportunity to choose a kitten from a round basket. Foolishly ignoring the Payne's Choice rules, I picked a tabby-and-white already named William, simply because he kept trying again to walk round the rim each time he fell off. He turned out to be a long-haired wimp.

Humour your addict by preparing a best-behaviour pattern of responses to interrogation from a fierce woman inspector who calls to make sure your home is suitable for fostering a rescued cat. No jokes, by request. It's more rigorous than adopting a child. And if the plan fails, you take the blame.

Never forget, though, that homing a pet animal has one great advantage over adopting a human baby: if medical treatment fails, a cat can expeditiously be put to sleep by the vet. There's a lot of fuss from doctors if you try to do that with human babies.

No-go Areas and All-round Defence

N ever forget that anything which inflicts even the slightest injury, or imagined injury, on a cat is strictly forbidden. Even a light finger tap to its nose can be enough to ruin inter-human household relations for days.

Beware of cats in the bathroom. Some display an unhealthy interest in lavatories. Others take a prurient delight in sneering at the absurd movements of naked humans disporting themselves in the bath.

Do not forget that a cat anywhere near a quantity of water is itself dicing with death. The dear creatures are in mortal terror of drowning, and it does no harm to remind them that in the long run their safety depends on you. They may have folk memories of drowning kittens.

Aversion therapy is a key item in the armoury of those among us forced by circumstance to ensure the good behaviour of rowdy creatures with twitching tails.

To copy the cat can be sound advice. They have no sense of guilt and survive by what we skilled psycho-handlers call distance control. In a nutshell, if they get the idea that you are hostile, they stay well away. There is no rule against humans doing the same to them.

One onerous though essential duty that falls upon the fanatic's companion is responsibility for maintaining law and order in what has inappropriately been called the feline community. Real pet-owners are far too unrealistic and tender-hearted to administer necessary retribution for misdemeanours.

Nor do cat fanatics have the steel necessary for warnings to pre-empt mischief. Anyway, such people almost always give the cat the benefit of the doubt in the face of manifest proof of bad behaviour:

'Just look at Gizmo patting that egg off the table – he's pretending it's a ball and he wants to play.'

Oh no he doesn't! He either just feels like raising hell or he wants more food.

Keep a loaded water pistol by you at all times. It may legitimately be used both for self-defence and for protecting quadruped loved ones against hostile enemies. Recommended weapons are the advanced models found in good toyshops that are capable of delivering a small jet of cold water at long range.

The LRWW, as the long-range water weapon is designated, may successfully be used to deter friendly cats intent on unlawful bird and small mammal kills. The moment to strike is when the cat moves into what we behaviourists call the 'predatory sequence' – stalk, pounce, kill, eat. A quick burst can halt it, even at risk of offending your fanatic.

To avoid owner trouble, attempt to fire from a concealed sniper position. SAS training can be useful here, though not essential. If caught, the fall-back justification is to plead undying love for birds in general and pretty songbirds in particular. Remind the fanatic of childhood affection for mice.

One useful form of passive defence (and an owner-approved one) is to keep handy a sealed jar of catnip leaves. When more aggressive measures fail, as they frequently do, give the malefactors a whiff of this powerful drug. They cannot get enough and roll about giggling like kids on hash.

Actions in the field of law-and-order maintenance are best considered as covert operations. One useful technique still available in less politically correct households is tobacco smoke blowing. A well-directed puff of old shag pipe tobacco is quite enough to put the boldest tom to flight. Failing that, healthy-life persons may prefer to squeeze oranges or lemons as a repellent.

For indoor trouble-prevention measures I recommend judicious use of a magazine thrown above the quadruped bad guy. Its pages flutter open as it falls, emulating the action of a diving bird of prey, without any of the unpleasant consequences of keeping an eagle about the house.

Intellectual political weeklies are particularly effective cat deterrents. The *Spectator* and the *New Statesman* have proved equally useful, regardless of their opposing political views. They can be obtained from any good newsagent. Use of fashion magazines such as *Vogue* cannot be recommended. They are far too

heavy for the purpose and con-
demned by Cats Protection folk.

Remember: cats themselves are
incapable of feeling guilt, so
never apologise. *Regrette rien*. They
will not hold it against you.

Give an Inch and Addicts Will Make Life Hell

Discourage from the very first outbreak any tendency to humanise cat conversation. It is not recommendable for grown-up persons to utter remarks like 'Come to mummy, kitty-witty.' In excess, use of such endearments can soften the brain. Always address cats formally in adult language.

Unless vigorous counter-measures are taken, the small co-resident creatures will dominate your life and control household decision-making. For instance, you plan to move house and what is concern number one? Is the garden adequately protected for the cats to feel at ease? Is the street too busy and dangerous?

The fanatic's companion can, of course, use cat anxieties to serve his own ends. Just to remark, 'I didn't like the look of that Rottweiler at the end of the street. Nasty bark,' is quite enough to forestall a house purchase there.

If there are cats about, abandon hope forever of enjoying a solitary reading dinner of cold meat and salad, lubricated with a glass or two of claret. Such a cold collation attracts the envy of the feline chum, who will leap on the table, lick its posterior, then sit on your paperback and stare intently until repeatedly given a piece of meat.

Get used to seeing claw marks in the butter dish where an alien tongue has already been at work.

It is in the nature of the beast to dislike and try to avoid any kind of travel. Cars, trains, aircraft, bicycles and boats are all marked down on a cat's banned list. In their eyes, locomotion is out. The keeper must either emulate the kept and stay at home for ever or engage in a fierce battle of wills to force them boxed into some form of transport.

The domestic enthusiast must be discouraged from cooing and making soothing noises at backseat feline drivers Any attempt to silence their protest in cars brings on a contrary effect by encouraging them to make ever more fiendish noises.

These animals have a nasty knack when angry or scared of peeing in cars. The smell from such vindictive exercises is virtually irremovable. It is well worth buying an old banger for the partner whose nose is desensitised by love.

For the truly worshipful owner, long holidays are out. It is a golden rule that the darling quadrupeds must never be left alone for more than a day or two, so forget those dreams of faraway places and golden beaches. The cat addict's perfect partner should be a totally boring stay-at-home person.

What you have chosen is what you get, as anxious short breaks replace long relaxations. They are punctuated with worries about whether the warders at the cat's hotel are being really kind and loving to the reluctant quadruped pensionnaires. Get used to the idea that your partner half believes that the beloved animals have been dispatched to Guantanamo Bay, yet still sends them holiday postcards – 'Miss you terribly, darling.'

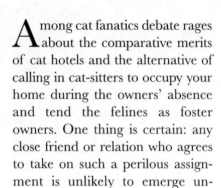

Among cat fanatics debate rages about the comparative merits of cat hotels and the alternative of calling in cat-sitters to occupy your home during the owners' absence and tend the felines as foster owners. One thing is certain: any close friend or relation who agrees to take on such a perilous assignment is unlikely to emerge unscathed.

If a minder has to be used, then the person selected will have to undergo a process of personal vetting normally demanded for recruits to the Secret Intelligence Service.

On the subject of the disadvantages of being connected to a cat devotee, permit me to point out also that, unlike dogs, cats cannot be taken for pleasant country walks. In exceptionally favourable circumstances, some do accompany their human companions a short way. Our tabby William will trot along with me for twenty metres or so before losing interest or becoming distracted by a passing gnat.

Like any time of celebration and holiday, Christmas is one of great stress brought on by fierce decision-making about presents for

the little sweethearts, and by what
is to become of them while we
'enjoy' ourselves. For those who are
not enthusiastic about the season,
simple amusement can be arranged
by secretly attaching 100 grams of
shrimps to a cat-loving neighbour's
Christmas tree. Then it's open
doors for the cats of the district to
do their worst.

The Home Life of
Our Own Dear Cat

Cats do furnish a room, several rooms in fact, or rather their loving owners do by endlessly responding to magazine ads: a mounting ramp to provide easy access to a favourite chair for your

stiff-legged moggie; a special electrically heated, rug-lined tunnel (a snip at only £59.65, in red, green or khaki); a special scratching post; or a waterbed for the old and arthritic. Such objects quickly crowd out human furniture and destroy the comforts of home.

If you ever want to sell the place, first send the addict away to a health spa and the cats to a cattery. Then detox the house. Clean it as thoroughly as the mafia do following a bout of family slaughter. Finally, all feline furniture and belongings should go into storage until the last viewer has viewed and you have safely banked the money. Thousands of pounds are at stake.

The other side of the coin is all the special measures that are needed to protect real grown-up furniture from assault by cruel, maliciously directed claws. Sticky tape sometimes deters them, but sharp-edged, mini tank traps screwed to chairs and tables are better.

To find out how hellish it is living in a cat's hospital, just wait for the little darling to fall sick. When our old moggie had her operation, she was forced to convalesce wearing a sort of plastic lampshade over her head to stop her scratching the healing wound. In a fit of temper she cut my hand with it.

In sickness and in health, the addict-management industry is no place for the faint-hearted or those easily upset by scenes of joint feline/human suffering. If anything, the sickness bit is the hardest to endure. A vomiting cat, or one bleeding after scratching its operation scars, is not a pretty sight. We must suffer in silence and do our best to keep the bloodstained patient well away from bed linen or best shirt.

A particularly difficult time for the partner of an enthusiast is the behaviour protocol to be followed after the passing over of a dearly loved quadruped. It goes without saying that suitable grief must be expressed, while care is taken to counsel against funereal excesses in the way of rosewood coffins, stone crosses and elaborate services. Keep it quick and simple.

Emotional electricity may safely be discharged by binning items of equipment of the defunct, such as a water bowl with their name painted on it, a favourite toy or a recent birthday gift. Otherwise, watch out for tear squalls when such items are discovered with cries of, 'I can't bear it! Look at his little bowl. He loved that bowl.'

Thought must be given to the choice of burial places, usually

in the garden. Burials at sea are rare
for creatures known to be so fearful
of the deep, the exception being
made for ships' cats. They desert
sinking ships well ahead of rats.
Although not keen on swimming,
the cats manage to hit the lifeboats
well before the first women and
children, and have time enough to
stamp their paws on the feet of rats
struggling to get onboard.

One owner had her husband's
ashes scattered over her cat's
grave so that she could keep an eye
on both of them – a practice not to
be recommended by partners of
either sex.

What we experts on cat-enthusiast behaviour refer to as the 'post-cat' depression period is a dangerous time for other reasons too. There is a strong tendency among cat freaks in mourning towards acquisitive behaviour. At the first sign of an attempt to replace the deceased, the human companion should rigorously ward off any such ideas. This is a good time to suggest a long holiday abroad.

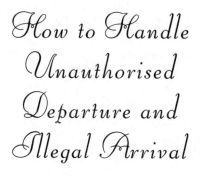

How to Handle Unauthorised Departure and Illegal Arrival

There are ferals at the bottom of our garden. There always are. After a cat death or other unauthorised departure, word soon spreads that a social security place has become available.

What the refugees from other areas are really after is an addict in search of a new lodger. For comfort, they prefer sole occupancy and hate cat-lovers who admit a whole houseful of strays. These are places that serious cat-home seekers avoid, except in an emergency.

A notice in the village store says: 'Albert is still missing, but he has been seen in West Avenue. If someone is feeding him and he has found a new home, would they please telephone us.' That is known as cat ingratitude to humans.

The Missing Cat Effect may bring disharmony in the household, sometimes – though not always – remedied with comments of controlled insouciance. 'He'll probably turn up later if we just go to bed and put the lights out,' is one useful phrase. Frankly, it does not hold up well against the cat lady's lament, 'I can just see his little body crushed under car wheels and/or torn by a fox.' Watch and pray.

The husband of a cat owner whose pets disappeared, untimely liberated at a motorway service station, was heard to say during the two-hour search, 'I hope they went to the road and got squashed.' That kind of reaction is neither correct nor helpful, and cannot be commended.

The cat, once a lonely hunter, is now more like a weekend shooter. They no longer kill for the pot as in happier times and even expect something a touch more gastronomic on returning home. 'Chicken and liver pâté, sir?' Or, 'A little cold fish with shrimp, madam?'

Try using the cat as a catalyst. For instance, take the heat out of a mother/daughter quarrel that's on the point of going critical by saying, 'Just look at that kitten scrambling up the oak tree.' Peace breaks out – well, sometimes.

Having myself sampled some of cats' tinned stuff on lonely nights when the human cupboard was Mother Hubbardish, I can testify that it's not bad tucker. Besotted owners shrink before no sacrifice to titillate the appetite of four-footed house guests.

Useful phrases to soothe the anxious cat-lover's troubled brow:

- 'That cat really loves you!'
- 'It's almost as if he could talk/ understand every word. He knows we are going away.'
- 'She's really happy in the new garden.'
- 'What a clever animal.'
- 'I think they really enjoy staying in that cats' hotel.'

Once you have learned to master this dreadful pussycat speak, you are accepted into the pet-

loving tendency that has its clan-
destine support groups everywhere.
But in the long stretches of nights
rendered sleepless by various catlike
activities, the mind can turn to
thoughts of self-liberation from this
eerie world. Divorce may be the
final solution.

There are several obvious danger indicators. The first becomes apparent when the partner
begins inviting ever more 'feline
guests' into the house. A second
animal may be accepted more or
less graciously. If it gets to the sixth
and seventh, it's time to start think-

ing about which items of furniture
to insist on keeping when the split
comes.

Cat Rescue Missions Can Damage Your Home Life

There are two 'Looney Tunes' categories of quantity cat collectors: the rescuers and the breeders. Members of the first group can hardly bear to wait for nightfall before setting off in search of unwitting ferals. Once trapped, they are rushed off to the nearest vet to be neutered and then foisted off upon unwilling new owners. 'It's for their own good,' is the cry. So human males beware!

Another practice to be on the alert for is attending or taking part in cat shows. Urged on by desire for a badge or a ribbon to prove conclusively that their cat is bigger, better and cleverer than others, the fanatic will spend hours grooming the wretched creature in smelly church halls or show tents.

The shrewd companion of a cat enthusiast must learn diversion techniques to prevent the casual acquisition of ready-for-rescue cats and kittens (RFRs, as they are known to us professionals) that appear miraculously by the side of motorways or in lay-bys. Develop the eye of a lynx to spot trouble ahead and accelerate fast, justifying your move if it is detected by outlining the dangers of emergency stops on crowded roads.

The worst case scenario in the matter of cat-rescue perils begins under the vine-leaved canopy of some charming Greek taverna or Spanish tapas joint. The food is delicious and the wine flows as a team of pretty, anorexic kittens enters stage left all set to excite compassion.

'They're so sweet. Look how hungry they are.' Then, as a waiter sends them packing, an operatically darker cry springs from your companion: 'Latins are so cruel to animals.'

There follow alarming demands to adopt the skinny things and take them home to a life of love and obesity in England. Take immediate action to pre-empt such a move by any means available – feign a heart attack, swoon, begin vomiting. Not only is rescuing foreign cats ruinously expensive – re-mortgage time, honey – but it also involves bureaucracy, anti-terror laws, quarantine boarding fees and finally vet bills. The Big Ks start looming.

Some feline fanatics specialise in rescuing disabled cats with three legs instead of the customary four. Their delight is to care for the halt and the lame, the blind and the deaf. All that is no doubt very admirable, and great if you don't mind converting your home into a battlefield forward dressing station, but it's no place for the hard-hearted. It's best for them (I mean, me) not to get involved, except to deploy imaginative reasons why not to do this.

There are those who carry around in their cars a whole larder of cat food ready to hand out just in case their tender heart happens to meet a starving cat. Others always keep a few cat treats in a handbag or pocket ready to dis-

pense instant charity. With so many do-gooders on the loose, it's amazing there are any hungry cats still to be found at all.

They who admit a cat or cats into their home must say adieu to gracious living. A cat's home soon becomes his cardboard castle.

Neurotic Cats and Owners, Their Name Is Legion

A garden is a lovesome thing, God wot. Under the malign influence of the nation's best-loved pet, it can turn into a loathsome thing. It may become a Colditz of electrified wire fencing to prevent escapes or to keep out feline troublemakers intent on attacking the resident darlings. Young trees clawed to pieces and rare plants scratched up by you-know-who help to create a 1914 front-line atmosphere. Keen gardeners should re-home themselves or look forward to an early death.

Cats cannot resist the temptation to drag into the human residence anything that has attracted their febrile and murderous attention. Dead mice, struggling small birds and mono-winged butterflies or worms are all mustered for human attention. Their game book is as thick as a Bible.

That is fine for your addict companion who, although theoretically a lover of all animals, will not only excuse such outrages but condone them by affecting to be a mummy cat receiving a kindly gift from the offspring. The required defence against such nonsense is to grab the gifts and bin them before more harm is done.

Like musical persons and mathematicians, cat folk have a very simple sense of humour. It is not unusual to watch a full-grown, intelligent woman laughing and giggling with pleasure as her fanatical friend administers a bout of clicker training to feline chums. In theory, every click accompanied with a food reward will induce the pet to roll over, sit up and beg, or 'die for Tony Blair'. Absurd! So be tolerant and wait for it to go away, unless there are signs that one's own clicker training has started.

Cat-lovers favour catflaps because they provide easy ingress and egress for felines on their lawful occasion. So does the thoughtful companion, namely me. Without them, a 24-hour door guard has to be mounted to handle continual cat demands to be let in or let out.

The catflap is a tricky accoutrement to handle and is quite likely to cause in-house discord. It is expensive to fit into doors and windows, especially double-glazed ones. Moreover, it cannot readily identify friend from foe. Hostile marauders get easy access to the sacred heartland territory of house cats. Worse may be yet to come. A cat on the loose can just wander in, decide it likes the look of the place and settle down in its new home, to the chagrin of those already installed.

Great theological battles divide the religion of cat worshippers. For instance, they argue incessantly about whether domestic cats should be forced to stay indoors at night or be pushed out into the dark. On questions of such high importance it is wise for those on the fringes to stay silent. The best advice is to follow the rule of the house made by the senior cat person, unless of course you are intent on making mischief.

Another big debate circles around whether or not foxes attack and kill cats. Avoid this contro-

versy at all costs and sidestep any
dealings with kind-hearted, far-out
cat ladies who still cling to the here-
tical belief that cats never kill birds.

Whatever became of my beautiful car, its bonnet scarred
with claw marks? Its windows now
are festooned with silly warning
boasts like 'Show Cats in Transit'
or, dafter still, 'Slow Down for Cats'
and 'Cats Are People Too'.

My very own cat-loving lady lied about fleas. They had no effect on humans, she said. Then, in the face of facts to the contrary, she mumbled about new evidence possibly having been discovered recently. Anyway, cats do have fleas. But when cats scratch themselves so fiendishly, it is not necessarily because of fleas.

Fleas are sometimes imaginary, for when it comes to neurotic cats, their name is legion. Anxieties may cause even the most loveable cat to tear out its fur, or leave unmentionable filth in human beds and spray urine. Alas, the cure is even worse, what with consultant pet psychiatrists and expensive cat counsellors. Pay up, pay up and play the game. Time to re-home either the minder or cats.

Count your blessings but keep your powder dry:

- No dressing-up clothes have been acquired to turn Miss Pussycat into a Christmas fairy.
- No special cat's pram has yet been mentioned.
- A designated pussy's garden remains a distant dream, mentioned but not proceeded with.

All the above also count as immediate danger signals, even though they come up only in casual conversation.

In an ideal world, pet cats would live in their own quarters, in pussy flats or granny-flat style. They would be brought into human areas, as Edwardian children used to be, to amuse the grown-ups for half an hour before dinner. Then catophiles could get a decent night's sleep.

Cats and Human Sex Life – Antidote or Aid to Seduction?

Keep cats out of the bedroom at all costs. Infuriating feline fascination with what the humans are up to must have spoiled more nights of passion than grey, flannel knickers ever did. The lithe and relaxed stretchings of a bedside cat depressingly emphasise the grotesque clumsiness of your own movements. In extreme cases, this may lead to male impotence.

If you are involved with felines yet favour the sleek, beautiful kind of mistress, well-dressed and elegant like Catherine Deneuve in *Belle du Jour*, forget it. Just look what the love of cats has done to Brigitte Bardot and you will begin to get the picture. Elegant stockings and fashionable skirts are the first victims of the four-foot hordes. Addicts wear messy old jeans and horrible pullovers embroidered with cat heads.

Young men at risk would do well to remember the Edwardian maiden's threat: 'Lips that touch pussycats' shall ne'er touch mine.'

'Who desires the daughter, admires and flatters the mother.' This useful maxim of old French boulevardiers bent on seduction may, in some cases, be adapted by present-day questing males intent on winning the affections of ladies with cats. A few points may be won for starters by some phrase such as: 'I think that is the most beautiful cat I have ever seen.' A bit of sensual fondling of the cat's ears begins to act as a come-on to the cat owner. It has been called four-paw foreplay.

The love of cats and kittens, sincerely felt by most addicts, can be exploited and transformed into love of fellow humans. So it is possible for the lover to make a path to the bedroom following the paw-steps of the cat.

Thought for the Day

Remember: the love of cats passeth all understanding and there's not a lot to be done about that.